'E Korai Biini

Baania: Fox Mono
Nunu baania: John Robert Azuelo
Edit baania: Margaret Saumore

Library For All Ltd.

'E Korai Biini

First published 2021

Published by Library For All Ltd
Email: info@libraryforall.org
URL: libraryforall.org

This book was made possible by the generous support of the Education Cooperation Program.

Original illustrations by John Robert Azuelo

'E Korai Biini
Fox Mono
ISBN: 978-1-922750-92-1
SKU01848

'E Korai Biini

'A mauru dioi ano.

'A rabasiai ano.

'A rabasiai sina.

'A rabasiai rangi.

'A rabasiai wai.

'A rabasiai aruwai.

Maagui rarai
ma raboaʻa.

Maagui raboa
ta'eha baaniai ano.

Maagui tahi raha
ma kakaroʻa suriai
moou.

Maagui hungu ma to'ora'i mwane huai biini.

You can use these questions to talk about this book with your family, friends and teachers.

What did you learn from this book?

Describe this book in one word. Funny? Scary? Colourful? Interesting?

How did this book make you feel when you finished reading it?

What was your favourite part of this book?

download our reader app
getlibraryforall.org

About the contributors

Bukani ra tagorahia goni beiai Ministri anai Edukeison mana Hiuman Risoses Development. 'Iraau ha'ausuri ni Arosi suri'i venakiula klas, na'i Arosi One, West Makira Constituency, Makira Ulawa Province na raau usu'i.

Did you enjoy this book?

We have hundreds more expertly curated original stories to choose from.

We work in partnership with authors, educators, cultural advisors, governments and NGOs to bring the joy of reading to children everywhere.

Did you know?

We create global impact in these fields by embracing the United Nations Sustainable Development Goals.

www.ingramcontent.com/pod-product-compliance
Lightning Source LLC
Chambersburg PA
CBHW040317050426
42452CB00018B/2897